MARKETING MANAGEMENT

A STRATEGIC DECISION-MAKING APPROACH

Alreck & Settle
The Survey Research Handbook
Third Edition

Anderson, Beveridge, Lawton & Scott
Merlin: A Marketing Simulation
First Edition

Arens
Contemporary Advertising
Ninth Edition

Arnould, Price & Zinkhan
Consumers
Second Edition

Bearden, Ingram & LaForge
Marketing: Principles & Perspectives
Fourth Edition

Belch & Belch
Advertising & Promotion: An Integrated Marketing Communications Approach
Sixth Edition

Bingham & Gomes
Business Marketing
Third Edition

Cateora & Graham
International Marketing
Twelfth Edition

Cole & Mishler
Consumer and Business Credit Management
Eleventh Edition

Cravens & Piercy
Strategic Marketing
Seventh Edition

Cravens, Lamb & Crittenden
Strategic Marketing Management Cases
Seventh Edition

Crawford & Di Benedetto
New Products Management
Seventh Edition

Duncan
Principles of Advertising and IMC
Second Edition

Dwyer & Tanner
Business Marketing
Second Edition

Eisenmann
Internet Business Models: Text and Cases
First Edition

Etzel, Walker & Stanton
Marketing
Thirteenth Edition

Forrest
Internet Marketing Intelligence
First Edition

Futrell
ABC's of Relationship Selling
Eighth Edition

Futrell
Fundamentals of Selling
Eighth Edition

Gourville, Quelch & Rangan
Cases in Health Care Marketing
First Edition

Hair, Bush & Ortinau
Marketing Research
Second Edition

Hawkins, Best & Coney
Consumer Behavior
Ninth Edition

Johansson
Global Marketing
Third Edition

Johnston & Marshall
Churchill/Ford/Walker's Sales Force Management
Seventh Edition

Johnston & Marshall
Relationship Selling and Sales Management
First Edition

Kerin, Hartley & Rudelius
Marketing: The Core
First Edition

Kerin, Berkowitz, Hartley & Rudelius
Marketing
Seventh Edition

Lehmann & Winer
Analysis for Marketing Planning
Fifth Edition

Lehmann & Winer
Product Management
Third Edition

Levy & Weitz
Retailing Management
Fifth Edition

Mason & Perreault
The Marketing Game!
Third Edition

McDonald
Direct Marketing: An Integrated Approach
First Edition

Mohammed, Fisher, Jaworski & Paddison
Internet Marketing: Building Advantage in a Networked Economy
Second Edition

Monroe
Pricing
Third Edition

Mullins, Walker & Boyd
Marketing Management: A Strategic Decision-Making Approach
Fifth Edition

Nentl & Miller
SimSeries Simulations:
   SimSell
   SimSales Management
   SimMarketing
   SimMarketing Research
   SimCRM
First Edition

Pelton, Strutton, Lumpkin & Cooper
Marketing Channels: A Relationship Management Approach
Third Edition

Perreault & McCarthy
Basic Marketing: A Global Managerial Approach
Fifteenth Edition

Perreault & McCarthy
Essentials of Marketing: A Global Managerial Approach
Ninth Edition

Peter & Donnelly
A Preface to Marketing Management
Ninth Edition

Peter & Donnelly
Marketing Management: Knowledge and Skills
Seventh Edition

MARKETING MANAGEMENT
A STRATEGIC DECISION-MAKING APPROACH

FIFTH EDITION

JOHN W. MULLINS
Associate Professor of Management Practice
London Business School

ORVILLE C. WALKER JR.
James D. Watkins Professor of Marketing, Emeritus
University of Minnesota

HARPER W. BOYD JR.
Donaghey Distinguished Professor of Marketing
University of Arkansas–Little Rock

JEAN-CLAUDE LARRÉCHÉ
Alfred H. Heineken Professor of Marketing
European Institute of Business Administration
INSEAD

McGraw-Hill
Irwin

Boston   Burr Ridge, IL   Dubuque, IA   Madison, WI   New York   San Francisco   St. Louis
Bangkok   Bogotá   Caracas   Kuala Lumpur   Lisbon   London   Madrid   Mexico City
Milan   Montreal   New Delhi   Santiago   Seoul   Singapore   Sydney   Taipei   Toronto

McGraw-Hill Irwin

MARKETING MANAGEMENT: A STRATEGIC DECISION-MAKING APPROACH

Published by McGraw-Hill/Irwin, a business unit of The McGraw-Hill Companies, Inc. 1221 Avenue of the Americas, New York, NY, 10020. Copyright © 2005, 2002, 1998, 1995, 1990, by The McGraw-Hill Companies, Inc. All rights reserved. No part of this publication may be reproduced or distributed in any form or by any means, or stored in a database or retrieval system, without the prior written consent of The McGraw-Hill Companies, Inc., including, but not limited to, in any network or other electronic storage or transmission, or broadcast for distance learning.

Some ancillaries, including electronic and print components, may not be available to customers outside the United States.

This book is printed on acid-free paper.

domestic   4 5 6 7 8 9 0 QPD/QPD 0 9 8 7 6
international   11 12 13 14 15 16 QPD/QPD 0 9 8 7 6

ISBN–13: 978–0–07–286370–3
ISBN–10: 0–07–286370–6

Vice president and editor-in-chief: *Robin J. Zwettler*
Editorial director: *John E. Biernat*
Sponsoring editor: *Barrett Koger*
Editorial assistant: *Jill M. O'Malley*
Media producer: *Craig Atkins*
Project manager: *Laura Griffin*
Production supervisor: *Gina Hangos*
Coordinator freelance design: *Artemio Ortiz Jr.*
Photo research coordinator: *Jeremy Cheshareck*
Photo researcher: *Kelly Mountain*
Lead supplement producer: *Cathy L. Tepper*
Senior digital content specialist: *Brian Nacik*
Cover and interior design: *Ryan Brown*
Typeface: *10/12 Times Roman*
Compositor: *GAC Indianapolis*
Printer: *Quebecor World Dubuque Inc.*

Library of Congress Cataloging-in-Publication Data

Mullins, John W. (John Walker)
    Marketing management : a strategic decision-making approach / John W. Mullins,
Orville C. Walker, Jr., Jean-Claude Larréché. — 5th ed.
        p. cm. — (McGraw-Hill/Irwin series in marketing)
    Rev. ed. of: Marketing management : a strategic, decision-making approach / Harper W.
Boyd, Jr. ... [et al.].
    ISBN 0-07-286370-6 (alk. paper)
        1. Marketing—Management. I. Walker, Orville C. II. Larréché, Jean-Claude. III.
Marketing management : a strategic, decision-making approach. IV. Title. V. Series.
HF5415.13.M845 2005
658.8—dc22
                                                                        20030066459

INTERNATIONAL EDITION ISBN–13: 978–0–07–111169–0   ISBN–10: 0–07–111169–7
Copyright © 2005. Exclusive rights by The McGraw-Hill Companies, Inc. for manufacture and export. This book cannot be re-exported from the country to which it is sold by McGraw-Hill. The International Edition is not available in North America.

www.mhhe.com

ABOUT THE AUTHORS

JOHN W. MULLINS

John W. Mullins is Associate Professor of Management Practice at London Business School, where he heads the entrepreneurship group. He earned his MBA at the Stanford Graduate School of Business and, considerably later in life, his Ph.D. in marketing from the University of Minnesota. An award-winning teacher, John brings to his teaching and research 20 years of executive experience in high-growth firms, including two ventures he founded, one of which he took public. Since becoming a business school professor in 1992, John has published more than 30 articles in a variety of outlets, including *Harvard Business Review*, the *Journal of Product Innovation Management*, and the *Journal of Business Venturing*. His research has won national and international awards from the Marketing Science Institute, the American Marketing Association, and the Richard D. Irwin Foundation. He is the author of *The New Business Road Test: What Entrepreneurs and Executives Should Do* Before *Writing a Business Plan*, and coauthor of *Marketing Strategy: A Decision-Focused Approach*, 4th edition.

ORVILLE C. WALKER JR.

Orville C. Walker Jr. is Professor Emeritus in the University of Minnesota's Carlson School of Management, where he served until recently as the James D. Watkins Professor of Marketing and Director of the Ph.D. Program. He holds a master's degree in social psychology from The Ohio State University and a Ph.D. in marketing from the University of Wisconsin–Madison. Orville has coauthored three books and has published more than 50 research articles in scholarly and business journals. He has won several awards for his research, including the O'Dell award from the *Journal of Marketing Research*, the Maynard award from the *Journal of Marketing*, and a lifetime achievement award from the Sales Management Interest Group of the American Marketing Association. Orville has been a consultant to a number of business firms and not-for-profit organizations, and he has taught in executive development programs around the world, including programs in Poland, Switzerland, Scotland, and Hong Kong. Perhaps his biggest business challenge, however, is attempting to turn a profit as the owner-manager of a small vineyard in western Wisconsin.

JEAN-CLAUDE LARRÉCHÉ

Jean-Claude Larréché is Alfred Heineken Professor of Marketing at the European Institute of Business Administration, INSEAD, in Fontainebleau, France. He holds an MBA from INSEAD and a Ph.D. from the Stanford Graduate School of Business. As a popular executive development teacher and consultant to major international firms, Jean-Claude has worked with top management teams in Europe, North America, and Asia. He is founder and chairman of StratX, a publisher of marketing simulations and other tools for strategic marketing. An award-winning teacher, Jean-Claude is also a two-time winner of the overall case competition of the European Case Clearing House, and coauthor of *Marketing Strategy: A Decision-Focused Approach*, 4th edition.

BRIEF CONTENTS

PREFACE   xviii

SECTION ONE

THE ROLE OF MARKETING IN DEVELOPING SUCCESSFUL BUSINESS STRATEGIES 1

1   The Marketing Management Process   2

2   The Marketing Implications of Corporate and Business Strategies   30

SECTION TWO

MARKET OPPORTUNITY ANALYSIS   65

3   Environmental Analysis: Tools to Identify Attractive Markets   66

4   Industry Analysis and Competitive Advantage   84

5   Understanding Consumer Buying Behavior   106

6   Understanding Organizational Markets and Buying Behavior   130

7   Measuring Market Opportunities: Forecasting and Marketing Research   152

8   Market Segmentation and Target Marketing   180

9   Differentiation and Positioning   200

SECTION THREE

DEVELOPING STRATEGIC MARKETING PROGRAMS   219

10   Business Strategies: A Foundation for Marketing Program Decisions   220

11   Product Decisions   242

12   Pricing Decisions   268

13   Distribution Channel Decisions   294

14   Integrated Promotion Decisions   326

SECTION FOUR

STRATEGIC MARKETING PROGRAMS FOR SELECTED SITUATIONS   353

15   Marketing Strategies for the New Economy   354

16   Strategies for New and Growing Markets   384

17   Strategic Choices for Mature and Declining Markets   418

SECTION FIVE

IMPLEMENTING AND CONTROLLING MARKETING PROGRAMS   447

18   Organizing and Planning for Effective Implementation   448

19   Measuring and Delivering Marketing Performance   474

INDEX   496

CONTENTS

PREFACE   xviii

SECTION ONE
THE ROLE OF MARKETING IN DEVELOPING
SUCCESSFUL BUSINESS STRATEGIES 1

1   The Marketing Management
    Process   2

RedEnvelope—Marketing Upscale Gifts Online   2
  A New Mission and Strategy   2
  The New Marketing Plan   2
  The Results   4

Marketing Challenges Addressed in Chapter 1   4

Why Are Marketing Decisions Important?   4
  The Importance of the Top Line   5

Marketing Creates Value by Facilitating Exchange
Relationships   5
  What Factors Are Necessary for a Successful
  Exchange Relationship?   6
  1. Who Markets and Who Buys? The Parties in
  an Exchange?   6
  2. Customer Needs and Wants   7
  3. What Gets Exchanged? Products and
  Services   10
  4. How Exchanges Create Value   10
  5. Defining a Market   12

What Does Effective Marketing Practice Look
Like?   13
  Marketing Management—A Definition   13
  Integrating Marketing Plans with the Company's
  Strategies and Resources   15
  Market Opportunity Analysis   16
  Formulating Strategic Marketing Programs   17
  Formulating Strategic Marketing Programs for
  Specific Situations   18
  Implementation and Control of the Marketing
  Program   19

The Marketing Plan—a Blueprint for
Action   20

Who Does What?   21
  Marketing Institutions   21
  Who Pays the Cost of Marketing Activities—and
  Are They Worth It?   22
  Room for Improvement in Marketing
  Efficiency   23
  The Role of the Marketing Decision Maker   24

Some Recent Developments Affecting Marketing
Management   24
  Globalization   25
  Increased Importance of Service   25
  Information Technology   25
  Relationships across Functions and Firms   27

Take-aways   27

Endnotes   28

2   The Marketing Implications of
    Corporate and Business
    Strategies   30

IBM Switches Strategies   30
  Technology Changes and Competitor Actions
  Require a Shift in Strategy   30
  A New Corporate Strategy   32
  New Business and Marketing Strategies   32
  The Bottom Line   33

Marketing Challenges Addressed in Chapter 2   33

What Is Marketing's Role in Formulating and
Implementing Strategies?   34
  Market-Oriented Management   35
  Does Being Market-Oriented Pay?   36
  Factors That Mediate Marketing's Strategic
  Role   37

Three Levels of Strategy: Similar Components, but
Different Issues   39

Strategy: A Definition   39
The Components of Strategy   40
The Hierarchy of Strategies   40
Corporate Strategy   40
Business-Level Strategy   42
Marketing Strategy   42

The Marketing Implications of Corporate Strategy
Decisions   42

Corporate Scope—Defining the Firm's
Mission   43
Corporate Objectives   46
Corporate Growth Strategies   48
Allocating Corporate Resources   51

The Marketing Implications of Business-Unit
Strategy Decisions   56

How Should Strategic Business Units Be
Designed?   58
The Business Unit's Objectives   58
The Business Unit's Competitive Strategy   58

Take-aways   60

Endnotes   61

Appendix 2.1 The American Marketing Association's
Code of Ethics   63

SECTION TWO
MARKET OPPORTUNITY ANALYSIS   65

**3   Environmental Analysis: Tools to
Identify Attractive Markets   66**

The Changing American Menswear Market   66

The Impact of Macroenvironmental Trends   66
What's Next? Will Suits Come Back?   67

Marketing Challenges Addressed in Chapter 3   67

Swimming Upstream or Downstream: An Important
Strategic Choice   68

Macro Trend Analysis: A Framework for Assessing
Market Attractiveness   68

The Demographic Environment   69
The Sociocultural Environment   70
The Economic Environment   72
The Political/Legal Environment   73
The Technological Environment   75
The Physical Environment   77

Environmental Analysis Guides Marketing Decision
Making   78

Prioritizing Trend Categories   78
Information Sources and Outputs of Macro
Trend Analysis   79
Anticipating and Responding to Environmental
Change   80

Take-aways   81

Endnotes   81

**4   Industry Analysis and Competitive
Advantage   84**

The Cellular Telephone Business: Increasing
Competition in a Growing Market   84

Cell Phone Manufacturing   84
Cell Phone Service Providers   84

Marketing Challenges Addressed in Chapter 4   85

Markets and Industries: What's the Difference?   85

Defining Markets and Industries: Levels of
Analysis   86
Challenges in Market and Industry
Definition   86

Your Market Is Attractive: What About Your
Industry?   88

Driving Forces   88
Porter's Five Competitive Forces   91
A Five Forces Analysis of the Cellular Phone
Service Industry   91
Changing Competition and Industry
Evolution   91
Critical Success Factors: Who Wins *within* an
Industry?   92

Industry Analysis Locally: How Intense Is the
Immediate Competition?   93

Rate of Diffusion of Innovations: Another Factor in
Assessing Opportunity Attractiveness   94

The Adoption Process   94
The Rate of Adoption   94
Adopter Categories   95
Implications of Diffusion of Innovation Theory
for Forecasting Sales of New Products and New
Firms   96

Sustaining Competitive Advantage over the Product
Life Cycle   97

A Forecaster's Toolkit: A Tool for Every Forecasting Setting   155

Statistical and Other Quantitative Methods   156
Observation   157
Surveys   157
Analogy   158
Judgment   159
Market Tests   159
Mathematics Entailed in Forecasting   160

Cautions and Caveats in Forecasting   161

Keys to Good Forecasting   161
Biases in Forecasting   162

Why Data? Why Marketing Research?   162

Market Knowledge Systems: Charting a Path toward Competitive Advantage   163

Internal Records Systems   163
Marketing Databases   164
Competitive Intelligence Systems   166
Client Contact and Salesforce Automation Systems   166
Other Kinds of Market Knowledge Systems   168

Marketing Research Resolves Specific Marketing Challenges   168

Step 1:   Identify the Managerial Problem and Establish Research Objectives   168
Step 2:   Determine the Data Sources and Types of Data Required   169
Step 3:   Design the Research   172
Step 4:   Collect the Data   174
Step 5:   Analyze the Data   175
Step 6:   Report the Results to the Decision Maker   175

What Users of Marketing Research Should Ask   176

Rudimentary Competence: Are We There Yet?   176

Take-aways   177

Endnotes   177

8   Market Segmentation and Target Marketing   180

Blue Ribbon Sports Targets Distance Runners   180

The Unique Needs of Distance Runners   180
The Waffle Revolution   180
Launching and Expanding the Nike Brand   181
World Cup 2002   181

Marketing Challenges Addressed in Chapter 8   181

Why Do Market Segmentation and Target Marketing Make Sense?   182

Most Markets Are Heterogeneous   182
Today's Market Realities Often Make Segmentation Imperative   183

How Are Market Segments Best Defined?   184

Demographic Descriptors   184
Geographic Descriptors   186
Geodemographic Descriptors   186
Behavioral Descriptors   187
Innovative Segmentation: A Key to Marketing Breakthroughs   189

Choosing Attractive Market Segments: A Five-Step Process   190

Step 1:   Select Market-Attractiveness and Competitive-Position Factors   191
Step 2:   Weight Each Factor   193
Step 3:   Rate Segments on Each Factor, Plot Results on Matrices   193
Step 4:   Project Future Position for Each Segment   194
Step 5:   Choose Segments to Target, Allocate Resources   195

Different Targeting Strategies Suit Different Opportunities   196

Niche-Market Strategy   197
Mass-Market Strategy   197
Growth-Market Strategy   197
Global Market Segmentation   197

Take-aways   198

Endnotes   198

9   Differentiation and Positioning   200

Repositioning French Wine   200

Marketing Challenges Addressed in Chapter 9   200

Differentiation: One Key to Customer Preference and Competitive Advantage   201

Differentiation in Business Strategies   202
Differentiation among Goods and Services   203

Physical Positioning   203

Limitations of Physical Positioning   204

Perceptual Positioning 204

Levers Marketers Can Use to Establish
Positioning 205

Preparing the Foundation for Marketing Strategies:
The Positioning Process 206

Step 1: Identify a Relevant Set of Competitive
Products 207
Step 2: Identify Determinant Attributes 207
Step 3: Collect Data about Customers'
Perceptions for Products in the Competitive
Set 209
Step 4: Analyze the Current Positions of
Products in the Competitive Set 209
Step 5: Determine Customers' Most Preferred
Combination of Attributes 211
Step 6: Consider Fit of Possible Positions
with Customer Needs and Segment
Attractiveness 212
Step 7: Write Positioning Statement or Value
Proposition to Guide Development of Marketing
Strategy 214

Analytical Tools for Positioning Decision
Making 216

Take-aways 218

Endnotes 218

Section Three
Developing Strategic Marketing Programs 219

10 Business Strategies: A Foundation for Marketing Program Decisions 220

Business Strategies and Marketing Programs
at 3M 220

Marketing Challenges Addressed in Chapter 10 221

How Do Businesses Compete? 223

Generic Business-Level Competitive
Strategies 223
Do the Same Competitive Strategies Work for
Single-Business Firms and Start-ups? 225
Do the Same Competitive Strategies Work for
Service Businesses? 226
Do the Same Competitive Strategies Work for
Global Competitors? 227

Will the Internet Change Everything? 228

How Do Competitive Strategies Differ from One
Another? 229

Differences in Scope 229
Differences in Goals and Objectives 230
Differences in Resource Deployments 231
Differences in Sources of Synergy 231

Deciding When a Strategy Is Appropriate:
The Fit between Business Strategies and the
Environment 232

Appropriate Conditions for a Prospector
Strategy 232
Appropriate Conditions for an Analyzer
Strategy 234
Appropriate Conditions for a Defender
Strategy 234

How Different Business Strategies Influence
Marketing Decisions 235

Product Policies 237
Pricing Policies 238
Distribution Policies 238
Promotion Policies 238

What If the Best Marketing Program for a
Product Does Not Fit the Business's Competitive
Strategy? 239

Take-aways 240

Endnotes 241

11 Product Decisions 242

Product Decisions in a Services Business 242

Marketing Challenges Addressed in Chapter 11 243

Product Design Decisions for Competitive
Advantage 244

Goods and Services: Are the Product Decisions
the Same? 245
Product Quality and Features Decisions 247
Branding Decisions 248
Packaging Decisions 251
Services Decisions and Warranties 251

Managing Product Lines for Customer Appeal and
Profit Performance 252

Line Filling 253
Line Stretching 254
Line Extensions 254

Brand Extensions   254
Dropping Products   255
Product Systems   255

New Product Development Process Decisions   255

The Importance of New Products to Long-Term
Profitability   256
New Product Success and Failure   256
Organizing for New Product Development   257
Key Decisions in the New Product Development
Process   258

Take-aways   265

Endnotes   266

12   Pricing Decisions   268

Ryanair: Low Prices but High Profits—So Far   268

Marketing Challenges Addressed in Chapter 12   269

A Process for Making Pricing Decisions   270

Strategic Pricing Objectives   270
Estimating Demand and Perceived Value   274
Estimating Costs   276
Analyzing Competitors' Costs and Prices   278

Methods Managers Use to Determine an Appropriate
Price Level   278

Cost-Oriented Methods   278
Competition-Oriented Methods   281
Customer-Oriented Methods   283

Deciding on a Price Structure: Adapting Prices to
Market Variations   286

Geographic Adjustments   286
Global Adjustments   287
Discounts and Allowances   288
Differential Pricing   290
Product-Line Pricing Adjustments   291

Take-aways   292

Endnotes   293

13   Distribution Channel Decisions   294

Changing Global Retail Trends Send a "Get Well"
Greeting to Hallmark   294

Marketing Challenges Addressed in Chapter 13   295

Why Do Multifirm Marketing Channels Exist?   296

Designing Distribution Channels: What Are the
Objectives to Be Accomplished?   297

Product Availability   299
Meeting Customers' Service Requirements   299
Promotional Effort   300
Market Information   300
Cost-Effectiveness   300
Flexibility   301

Designing Distribution Channels: What Kinds of
Institutions Might Be Included?   301

Merchant Wholesalers   301
Agent Middlemen   302
Retailers   302
Nonstore Retailing   303

Channel Design Alternatives   305

Alternative Consumer Goods Channels   305
Alternative Industrial Goods Channels   306

Which Alternative Is Best? It Depends on the Firm's
Objectives and Resources   307

Availability and the Satisfaction of Customer
Service Requirements   307
Promotional Effort, Market Information, and
Postsale Service Objectives   309
Cost-Effectiveness   310
Flexibility   312
Multichannel Distribution   312

Channel Design for Global Markets   313

Market Entry Strategies   313
Channel Alternatives   314

Channel Design for Services   315

Channel Management Decisions   316

Vertical Marketing Systems   316
Sources of Channel Power   319
Channel Control Strategies   320
Trade Promotions—Incentives for Motivating
Channel Members   321
Channel Conflicts and Resolution
Strategies   323

Take-aways   324

Endnotes   325

**14   Integrated Promotion
Decisions   326**

Integrated Marketing Communication Takes on Some
New Twists   326

Larazade   326

Big Brother   326
What's Next?   327

Marketing Challenges Addressed in Chapter 14   327

The Promotion Mix: A Communication Toolkit   328

Developing an Integrated Marketing
Communications Plan   329

Step 1:   Define the Audience(s) to Be
Targeted   329
Step 2:   Set the Promotional Objectives   330
Step 3:   Set the Promotion Budget   331
Step 4:   Design the Promotion Mix   332
Step 5:   Evaluate the Results   333

The Nitty-Gritty of Promotional Decision
Making   334

Making Advertising Decisions   334
Making Personal Selling Decisions   344
Organizing the Sales Effort in Global
Markets   344
Customer Service: An Increasingly Important
Personal Selling Function   346

Using Technology to Enhance Sales and Customer
Service Performance   347

Recruiting, Training, and Compensating Salespeople:
The Keys to Salesforce Performance   348

Evaluating and Controlling Salesforce Performance
to Ensure Delivery of Budgeted Results   348

Making Sales Promotion Decisions   349
Making Public Relations Decisions   350

Take-aways   351

Endnotes   351

SECTION FOUR
STRATEGIC MARKETING PROGRAMS FOR SELECTED
SITUATIONS   353

15   Marketing Strategies for the New
Economy   354

Chocolate Company Sweetens the Web   354

Thorntons Goes Online   354
Sweet Rewards   354

Marketing Challenges Addressed in Chapter 15   355

Does Every Company Need a New-Economy
Strategy?   356

Threats or Opportunities? The Inherent Advantages
and Disadvantages of the New Economy for
Marketers   358

The Syndication of Information   358
Increasing Returns to Scale of Network
Products   359
The Ability to Efficiently Personalize and
Customize Market Offerings   360
Disintermediation and Restructuring of
Distribution Channels   361
Global Reach, 24×7 Access, and Instantaneous
Delivery   361
Are These New-Economy Attributes
Opportunities or Threats?   362
First-Mover Advantage: Fact or Fiction?   365

Developing a New-Economy Strategy: A Decision
Framework   365

Marketing Applications for New-Economy
Tools   366
Developing New-Economy Marketing
Strategies: The Critical Questions   375

Developing Strategies to Serve New-Economy
Markets   378

What Lessons Can We Learn from the Dot.com
Crash?   379
What Are the Key Success Factors in Serving the
Dot.com Markets of Tomorrow?   380

Take-aways   382

Endnotes   382

16   Strategies for New and Growing
Markets   384

Canon, Inc.—Success That Is Hard to Copy   384

Marketing Challenges Addressed in Chapter 16   385

How New Is New?   386

Market Entry Strategies: Is It Better to Be a Pioneer
or a Follower?   388

Pioneer Strategy   388
Not All Pioneers Capitalize on Their Potential
Advantages   390
Follower Strategy   390
Determinants of Success for Pioneers and
Followers   391

Strategic Marketing Programs for Pioneers   393

Mass-Market Penetration   393

Niche Penetration   395
Skimming and Early Withdrawal   395
Marketing Program Components for a Mass-
Market Penetration Strategy   396
Marketing Program Components for a Niche
Penetration Strategy   400
Marketing Program Components for a Skimming
Strategy   400

Growth-Market Strategies for Market Leaders   401

Marketing Objectives for Share Leaders   401
Marketing Actions and Strategies to Achieve
Share-Maintenance Objectives   402
Fortress, or Position Defense, Strategy   402
Flanker Strategy   406
Confrontation Strategy   407
Market Expansion   408
Contraction or Strategic Withdrawal   408

Share-Growth Strategies for Followers   409

Marketing Objectives for Followers   409
Marketing Actions and Strategies to Achieve
Share Growth   409
Frontal Attack Strategy   411
Leapfrog Strategy   413
Flanking and Encirclement Strategies   414
Supporting Evidence   415

Take-aways   416

Endnotes   417

**17   Strategic Choices for Mature and
Declining Markets   418**

Johnson Controls—Making Money in Mature
Markets   418

Marketing Challenges Addressed in Chapter 17   419

Challenges in Mature Markets   420
Challenges in Declining Markets   420

Strategic Choices in Mature Markets   420

Strategies for Maintaining Competitive
Advantage   421
Methods of Differentiation   422
Methods of Maintaining a Low-Cost
Position   427
Customers' Satisfaction and Loyalty Are Crucial
for Maximizing Their Lifetime Value   429

Marketing Strategies for Mature Markets   431

Strategies for Maintaining Current Market
Share   431

Strategies for Extending Volume Growth   433

Strategies for Declining Markets   438

Relative Attractiveness of Declining
Markets   439
Divestment or Liquidation   441
Marketing Strategies for Remaining
Competitors   441

Take-aways   445

Endnotes   445

SECTION FIVE
**IMPLEMENTING AND CONTROLLING MARKETING
PROGRAMS   447**

**18   Organizing and Planning for Effective
Implementation   448**

Hewlett-Packard—Reorganizing to Implement a New
Strategy   448

The Internet Changed the Firm's Market
Environment   448
Reorganizing to Implement a New
Strategy   449

Marketing Challenges Addressed in Chapter 18   450

Designing Appropriate Administrative Relationships
for the Implementation of Different Competitive
Strategies   451

Business-Unit Autonomy   452
Shared Programs and Facilities   453
Evaluation and Reward Systems   454

Designing Appropriate Organizational Structures
and Processes for Implementing Different
Strategies   454

Functional Competencies and Resource
Allocation   455
Additional Considerations for Service
Organizations   455
Organizational Structures   457
Recent Trends in Organizational Design   461
Organizational Adjustments as Firms Grow and
Markets Change   462
Organizational Designs for Selling in Global
Markets   463

Marketing Plans: The Foundation for Implementing
Marketing Actions   465

The Situational Analysis   468

Key Issues   470
Objectives   470
Marketing Strategy   470
Action Plans   470
Projected Profit-and-Loss Statement   471
Contingency Plans   471

Take-aways   471

Endnotes   472

19   Measuring and Delivering Marketing Performance   474

Controls Pay for Wal-Mart   474

Marketing Challenges Addressed in Chapter 19   475

Designing Control Systems Step by Step   476

Setting Standards of Performance   477
Specifying and Obtaining Feedback Data   482
Evaluating Feedback Data   482
Taking Corrective Action   483

Design Decisions for Strategic Control Systems   484

Identifying Key Variables   484

Tracking and Monitoring   485
Strategy Reassessment   485

Design Decisions for Marketing Performance Measurement   486

Who Needs What Information?   486
When and How Often Is the Information Needed?   489
In What Media and in What Format(s) or Levels of Aggregation Should the Information Be Provided?   490
What Contingencies Should Be Planned For?   490
Global Marketing Control   492

A Tool for Periodic Assessment of Marketing Performance: The Marketing Audit   493

Types of Audits   493

Take-aways   495

Endnotes   495

INDEX   496

PREFACE

WHY THIS BOOK?

WHY DID YOUR INSTRUCTOR CHOOSE THIS BOOK? Chances are, it was for one or more of the following reasons:

- Among your instructor's objectives is to give you the necessary tools and frameworks to enable you to be an effective contributor to marketing decision making—regardless of whether you follow a career in marketing positions *per se*, in another functional area, or as an entrepreneur or in other general management roles. This book's focus on **strategic decision making** sets it apart from other texts that place greater emphasis on *description* of marketing phenomena than on the strategic and tactical marketing *decisions* that managers and entrepreneurs must make each and every day.

- Your instructor wants to use the most current and most **Internet-savvy** book available. We integrate the latest developments in Internet-based communication and distribution technology into every chapter, and we devote an entire chapter, Chapter 15, to the development of marketing strategies for the new economy. In addition, we supplement the book with an interactive website to help you self-test what you learn and to help your instructor choose the best cases and other materials and in-class activities.

   Although the stock market bubble built on dot.com start-ups burst several years ago, the proportion of goods and services marketed over the Internet continues to grow rapidly around the world. And increasing numbers of dot.com start-ups are finally achieving profitability. Therefore, our goal—and probably that of your instructor as well—is to make both the latest Internet-based tools as well as time-tested marketing principles relevant to those of you who will work in either old- or new-economy companies.

- Your instructor appreciates and believes you will benefit from the **real-world, global perspectives** offered by the authors of this book. Our combined entrepreneurial, marketing management, and consulting experience spans a broad variety of manufacturing, service, software, and distribution industries and has taken us—and thereby you, the reader—around the world many times.

As the reader will see from the outset in Chapter 1, marketing decision making is a critical activity in every firm, from start-ups to big companies with traditional marketing departments. Further, it is not just marketing managers who make marketing decisions. People in nearly every role in every company can have powerful influence on how happy customers are, or are not, with the goods and services the company provides. Stockbrokers must attract new customers. Accounting and consulting firms must find ways to differentiate their services from other providers so their customers have reasons to give them their business. Software engineers must understand how their technology can benefit the intended customer, for without such benefits, customers will not buy. Thus, we have written this book to meet the marketing needs of readers who hope to make a difference in the long-term strategic success of their organizations—whether their principal roles are in marketing or otherwise.

In this brief preface, we want to say a bit more about each of the three distinctive benefits, listed above, that this book offers its readers. We also point out the key changes in this edition compared to previous ones; and we thank our many students, colleagues, and others from whom we have learned so much, without whom this book would not have been possible.

A FOCUS ON STRATEGIC DECISION MAKING

Previous editions of this book have been known for their strategic approach, an approach that helps clarify the relationships among corporate, business-level, and marketing strategies for firms large and small; the

relationships between marketing strategies and the marketing environment; and the relationships between marketing and other functional areas in the firm. This fifth edition retains this strategic perspective while providing the reader with specific tools and frameworks for making marketing decisions that take best advantage of the conditions in which the firm finds itself—both internally, in terms of the firm's mission and competencies, and externally, in terms of the market and competitive context in which it operates.

This decision-focused approach is important to students and executives who are our readers, because, in most marketing management classes and executive courses, the students or participants will be asked to make numerous decisions—decisions in case studies about what the protagonist in the case should do; decisions in a course project, such as those entailed in developing a marketing plan; or decisions in a marketing simulation.

Our decision-focused approach is also important to employers, who tell us they want today's graduates to be prepared to "hit the ground running" and contribute to the firm's decision making from day one. The ability to bring thoughtful and disciplined tools and frameworks—as opposed to seat-of-the-pants hunches or blind intuition—to marketing decision making is one of the key assets today's business school graduates offer their employers. This book puts the tools in the toolbox to make this happen. In the end, employers want to know what their new hires can *do*, not just what they *know*.

WEB-SAVVY INSIGHTS

This book brings a realistic and informed perspective to an important question many students are asking: "Has the advent of the Internet changed all the rules?" Our answer is, "Well, yes and no." On one hand, the Internet has made available a host of new marketing tools, from banner ads to e-mail marketing to delivery of digital goods and services over the Internet, all of which are available to companies in the so-called old and new economies alike. On the other hand, time-tested marketing fundamentals, such as understanding one's customers and competitors and meeting customer needs in ways that are differentiated from the offerings of those competitors, have become even more important in the fast-moving digital world, as the many recent dot.com failures attest.

Thus, throughout the book, we integrate examples of new-economy companies—both successful and otherwise—to show how both yesterday's and today's marketing tools and decision frameworks can most effectively be applied. Because the advent of the Internet, mobile telephony, and other new-economy technologies is so important in its own right, however, we also devote Chapter 15 to new-economy strategies. This chapter provides for marketers in all kinds of companies a road map for decisions about where, when, and how to deploy new-economy tools.

A REAL-WORLD, GLOBAL PERSPECTIVE

Theory is important, because it enhances our understanding of business phenomena and helps managers think about what they should do. It is in the *application* of theory—the world of marketing practice—where we believe this book excels. Our decision focus is all about application. But we don't just bring an academic perspective to the party, important as that perspective is.

Two of us on the author team, Jean-Claude Larréché and John Mullins, have started successful entrepreneurial companies. One of these firms has "gone public." Two of us, Orv Walker and John, have worked in the United States, at the University of Minnesota and University of Denver, respectively. Two, Jean-Claude and John, work in Europe, Jean-Claude at INSEAD and John at the London Business School. All of us, including Harper Boyd, who passed away in 1999 but whose legacy lives on in this edition, have contributed the fruits of our research to the growing body of knowledge in the marketing management, marketing strategy, new products, and entrepreneurship arenas. The result of our collective and varied experience and expertise is a book filled with examples of real people from around the world making real decisions, examples of start-ups and high-growth companies as well as the more common examples of larger, more established firms.

WHAT'S NEW IN THIS EDITION?

Compared to the extensive changes we undertook last time, the revisions in this edition are largely a matter of fine-tuning rather than major restructuring. But no

chapter escaped untouched. All have been updated with the most recent marketing tools, techniques, and examples, although the basic flow, sequence, and strategic focus of the book have remained unchanged. We did, however, make a couple more extensive changes worth noting to those familiar with previous editions.

- Many of the new examples we have added throughout the book were chosen for the express purpose of increasing its global focus and international perspective. We have made an extensive effort to find and incorporate examples of marketing strategies and actions from firms and not-for-profit organizations all around the world, not just in the United States. Even many of the extensive case vignettes that open each chapter now focus on firms in Europe, Asia, and Africa.

- We have combined the two former chapters discussing promotion decisions and personal selling decisions into a single chapter that examines the choices involved in designing integrated marketing communications programs. Our rationale was simple: We think integrated communications programs can be understood best when the various components of such programs, together with their strengths and shortcomings, are examined in an integrated way within a single comprehensive chapter.

THANKS!

Simply put, this book is not solely our work—far from it. Many of our students, colleagues, and those we work with in industry have made contributions that have significantly shaped our perspectives on marketing decision making. We are grateful to all of them.

There are several people, though, who have played more direct roles in making this edition what it is, by providing detailed and constructive suggestions on one or more chapters or by helping us develop the related materials that make this book readable and useful for students and instructors alike. They include:

- Rhonda Bakke, Flathead Valley Community College–Kalispell
- Sarah Hickey, London Business School
- Nicola Lee, London Business School
- Nancy Jane Marlow, Eastern Illinois University
- Abi Murthy, London Business School
- Prema Nakra, Marist College
- Rosalyn S. Rufer, SUNY Empire State College
- Khaled Sartawi, Fort Valley State University

We also thank a small army of talented people at McGraw-Hill/Irwin for their work that has turned our rough manuscript into an attractive and readable book. In particular, our editors, Barrett Koger, Sarah Crago, and Jill O'Malley, have been instrumental in giving birth to this edition. Without them, we'd probably still be writing!

Finally, we thank Harper Boyd, without whom this book would not exist, and our parents, without whom, of course, none of us would be here. To all of you we extend our love, our respect, and our gratitude for passing on to us your curiosity and your passion for learning. We therefore dedicate this book to Harper Boyd, to Jeannette and Orville Walker, Sr., to Alice and Jack Mullins, and to Odette and Pierre Larréché.

John W. Mullins
Orville C. Walker Jr.
Jean-Claude Larréché
London, Minneapolis, and Fontainebleau
Summer 2003